DEVELOPMENT OF THREE COGNITIVE ASSESSMENTS FOR OFFICER CLASSIFICATION

CHELSEA BYRD

NIMBLE BOOKS LLC: THE AI LAB FOR BOOK-LOVERS

~ FRED ZIMMERMAN, EDITOR ~

Humans and AI making books richer, more diverse, and more surprising.

PUBLISHING INFORMATION

(c) 2024 Nimble Books LLC
ISBN: 978-1-60888-283-0

AI-GENERATED KEYWORD PHRASES

development and validation; cognitive assessments; officer classification; Systems Thinking assessment; Problem Solver assessment; Multitasking assessment; expert ratings; pilot test; discrimination capabilities; item development process; item types; scoring methods; construct; potential modifications; further research

PUBLISHER'S NOTES

Readers should read this document because it provides valuable insights into the development of cognitive assessments that measure important skills like systems thinking, problem-solving, and multitasking. These skills are crucial for officers in today's complex and fast-paced military environment, and understanding their development can contribute to the overall effectiveness of the Army. With the increasing demand for individuals who can navigate complex systems and solve problems effectively, this document offers valuable information for anyone interested in talent assessment and workforce development in our rapidly changing world.

Readers with military experience may form their own judgments about the efficacy of these techniques in the real world.

This annotated edition illustrates the capabilities of the AI Lab for Book-Lovers to add context and ease-of-use to manuscripts. It includes several types of abstracts, building from simplest to more complex: TLDR (one word), ELI5, TLDR (vanilla), Scientific Style, and Action Items; essays to increase viewpoint diversity, such as Grounds for Dissent, Red Team Critique, and MAGA Perspective; and Notable Passages and Nutshell Summaries for each page.

ANNOTATIONS

ABSTRACTS

TL;DR (ONE WORD)

Assessments.

EXPLAIN IT TO ME LIKE I'M FIVE YEARS OLD

This document is about tests that were made to see how well police officers can think, solve problems, and do multiple things at once. Experts looked at the tests and tried them out to see if they were good. The results showed that the tests were okay at telling the difference between officers who were good at these things and officers who weren't. The document also talks about how the tests were made and how they were scored. It also suggests ways to make the tests better and things that could be studied

TL;DR (VANILLA)

This document discusses the development and validation of three cognitive assessments for officer classification. The assessments were evaluated through expert ratings and a pilot test, showing reasonable discrimination capabilities. The document provides details on item development, scoring methods, and suggests areas for improvement and further research.

SCIENTIFIC STYLE

In this study, we developed and validated three cognitive assessments (Systems Thinking, Problem Solver, and Multitasking) for officer classification. The assessments were evaluated through expert ratings and a pilot test. The results indicated reasonable discrimination capabilities and provided valuable insights for improvement. We describe the item development process, including the item types and scoring methods for each construct. Additionally, we discuss potential modifications and areas for further research.

ACTION ITEMS

Review the expert ratings and pilot test results to identify areas for improvement in the cognitive assessments.

Consider making modifications to the assessments based on the insights gained from the evaluation process.

Conduct further research to validate and refine the assessments, potentially including additional pilot tests or expert ratings.

Continuously monitor and update the assessments as needed based on new research findings or changes in job requirements.

VIEWPOINTS

These perspectives increase the reader's exposure to viewpoint diversity.

GROUNDS FOR DISSENT

Lack of Validity: A member of the organization might have principled, substantive reasons to dissent from this report if they believe that the cognitive assessments described lack validity. They may argue that the expert ratings and pilot test used to evaluate the assessments were not comprehensive enough to truly assess their effectiveness. They might also question whether the assessments accurately measure the desired constructs of Systems Thinking, Problem Solver, and Multitasking. If they believe that the assessments do not provide valid results, it would be a principled reason for dissenting from the report.

Bias in Item Development: Another reason for dissent could be concerns about bias in the item development process. The member might argue that certain items or scoring methods were designed in a way that favors or disadvantages certain individuals or groups. For example, they may claim that the assessments place undue emphasis on skills or knowledge that are more prevalent among certain demographics, potentially leading to unfair outcomes or discriminatory practices. If they genuinely believe that bias exists in the item development process, it would be a substantive reason for dissent.

Insufficient Evidence for Improvement: A member might disagree with the report's suggestion of potential modifications and areas for further research due to a perceived lack of evidence supporting these suggestions. They may argue that without substantial data demonstrating the effectiveness of proposed modifications or areas for research, implementing them could be wasteful or even detrimental to the organization's goals. If they find the recommendations lacking evidential support, it would be a principled reason for dissenting from the report.

Ethical Concerns: Principled reasons for dissent could also arise from ethical concerns related to the assessments' impact on officers' careers. A member might contend that using such cognitive assessments as a basis for officer classification could lead to unintended consequences, such as unfairly limiting career prospects for qualified individuals who may struggle with specific aspects of Systems Thinking, Problem Solving, or Multitasking. They might argue that the assessments fail to consider other important qualities, such as leadership skills or emotional intelligence, which could be vital for effective performance. If they believe that the assessments have potential negative impacts on individuals' careers or fail to capture essential qualities, it would be a substantive reason for dissent.

Overall, principled and substantive reasons for dissent from this report could stem from concerns about validity, bias, lack of evidence for improvement suggestions, or ethical considerations related to career impact and the holistic assessment of officer capabilities.

RED TEAM CRITIQUE

Overall, the document provides a comprehensive overview of the development and validation process for three cognitive assessments: Systems Thinking, Problem Solver, and Multitasking. However, there are several areas that could benefit from further elaboration and improvement.

Firstly, the document briefly mentions expert ratings as part of the evaluation process but fails to provide any details on how these ratings were obtained or their specific relevance to the assessments. It would be helpful to include information on how these experts were selected, what criteria they used for rating each assessment, and whether their expertise aligns with the intended target audience.

Additionally, while the pilot test results indicate reasonable discrimination capabilities for all three assessments, it would be beneficial to have more specific information on what constitutes "reasonable" in this context. Providing statistical measures such as mean scores or standard deviations would enhance our understanding of how well each assessment performed during this initial testing phase.

Moreover, although the document outlines item development processes for each construct, it lacks specific examples or illustrations of items used in these assessments. Including sample items would not only help readers better grasp what is being assessed but also provide an opportunity to evaluate if certain items adequately measure desired skills or competencies.

Furthermore, while potential modifications and areas for further research are suggested towards the end of the document, they appear quite vague in nature. Expanding on these recommendations by providing more concrete suggestions or hypotheses for future investigations would be valuable. For instance, specifying which aspects of each assessment could potentially be improved or exploring alternative scoring methods could guide researchers interested in building upon this work.

Lastly, there seems to be limited discussion about potential limitations or biases associated with this study. It is important to acknowledge any possible sources of error or bias that may have influenced results and interpretations. Discussing such limitations will enhance transparency and ensure a more thorough critique of the validity and generalizability of findings.

In conclusion,

while this document serves as a robust starting point for developing cognitive assessments for officer classification, additional information and refinement in certain areas would elevate its rigor and overall usefulness. Strengthening the expert rating process, providing more specific details on pilot test results, including sample items, elaborating on potential modifications and areas of further research, and acknowledging any limitations or biases will enhance the value of this document as a guide for future work in this field.

MAGA PERSPECTIVE

This document is just another example of the liberal elite trying to control every aspect of our lives. Now they want to determine who can be an officer based on some fancy cognitive assessments. But what about real-life experience? It's clear that these so-called "experts" have no idea what it takes to be a good officer.

The fact that these assessments were validated through expert ratings is a red flag in itself. Who are these so-called experts and why should we trust their judgment? We all know that experts are often out of touch with everyday Americans, and their ratings are biased towards their own liberal agenda.

And let's talk about this pilot test. How do we know that it was conducted fairly and without any bias? I bet they cherry-picked participants who would perform well on these assessments, just to make them look good. This whole process reeks of manipulation and deceit.

Furthermore, the document suggests potential modifications and areas for further research, which only means one thing - they're not even sure if these assessments are accurate or effective. So why are they wasting our time and taxpayer money on something that may not even work?

In the end, this document is just another attempt by the left to undermine our law enforcement officers. They want to replace experienced officers with those who can pass some arbitrary tests, simply because it aligns with their own progressive agenda. Well, we won't stand for it. We need officers who understand the real world, not ones who excel in some academic assessment.

PAGE-BY-PAGE SUMMARIES

NOTABLE PASSAGES

BODY-10   "In the Systems Thinking measure, test takers demonstrate their understanding of the relationships and dynamics in systems by responding to a series of multiple-choice items that describe the relationships between or among elements of a system."

BODY-12   "The tasks needed to be detailed enough that the test taker would have to concentrate and focus in order to answer the questions about the content correctly, but simple enough that each item could be completed rather quickly. Another major consideration was to ensure the distractor task was sufficiently different from the primary task that it would require the test taker to mentally 'switch' between tasks."

BODY-20   "Item difficulties were calculated by examining the proportion of people who answered each question correctly out of the total number of people answering the question; that is, items for which fewer people answered correctly are considered to be more difficult. Results indicated that there were 10 very easy items (27%), which were answered correctly by 90-100% of the participants, and nine additional items (24%) that were answered correctly by 80-89% of participants. Only a small percentage of items were very high in difficulty, with three items (8%) that were answered correctly by fewer than half of participants."

BODY-24   "Participants performed more poorly on Approaches items than they did on Representation items. Scores ranged from 40% to 67% on the Approaches subscale and from 38% to 81% on the Representation subscale."

BODY-25   "Item difficulties were calculated by examining the proportion of people who answered the question correctly out of the total number of people answering the question. Results indicated that participants generally found the items to be difficult with 41% of items being answered correctly by less than half of participants."

BODY-26   "In general, the Problem Solver distractor response options were reasonably appealing to participants. The distribution of the number of distractors selected was negatively skewed, with participants selecting none of the distractors provided for only two of the items, and all three distractors for 10 of the items (see Table 14). For one item (Item 3), 17 participants selected the same distractor option, two participants each selected one of the other two distractor options, and zero participants selected the correct option. In total, there were four items (Items 3, 5, 23, and 34) that demonstrated this pattern, in which one response option dominated and few or no."

BODY-33   "In the second scoring approach used to calculate performance decrement, the subject's accuracy on the two items preceding each Distractor task was compared to their accuracy on the two items following each Distractor task. The average of the difference in performance was then calculated. This scoring approach resulted in almost half of participants (48%) demonstrating a 1%-15% increase in performance, and only 10% of participants demonstrating a 10%-20% performance decrement. Most of the remaining scores (42%) showed either no change (5 scores or 26% with 0% change) or a slight decrease in performance (3 scores or 16% with a 1-4% decrease)."

BODY-36   "Systems Thinking is a highly complex cognitive skill that has many knowledge and skill components. With the current measure we were specifically striving to capture whether individuals could conceptualize and understand relationships and arrangements within and between relevant components and structures."

BODY-37   *"Successful problem solving requires possessing a breadth of knowledge, and conceptually the items were striving to represent a broad spectrum of types of problems that may be encountered. As such, lower correlations among items would be desirable for this measure. Because the majority of the item total correlations were nonsignificant due to the very small sample size, speculation regarding the negative direction of the correlations is not worthwhile at this time; however, it could potentially suggest that being good at one type of problem approach or representation actually interferes with success in another type of approach or representation."*

BODY-38   *"In the end, our objective is to identify 12 items each for Approaches and Representation that can discriminate well among individuals. Using the current data, for the Approaches scale, if 6 items with the highest difficulty (Items 3, 5, 12, and 15) and lowest difficulty (Items 7 and 18) are dropped, the difficulties of the remaining items range from 37% to 89%, with an average difficulty of 61% across the remaining 12 items. For Representation, if items with the highest difficulty (Item 23, 30, 34, 36) and lowest difficulty (Items 25, 31) are dropped, the difficulties would range from 37% to79*

BODY-39   *"Study 2 results showed that the first measurement approach, which measured multitasking through comparison of the baseline performance to the interrupted performance, operated as expected, with most participants showing at least a 10% decrement in performance with the addition of interruptions. These results suggest that this general approach to measuring Multitasking is potentially effective; we were able to identify a performance decrement due to the Distractor task, and though variability was small, there was differentiation among participants in the performance decrement."*

BODY-40   *"While the investigation into the validity of Systems Thinking, Problem Solver, and Multitasking was very preliminary, results suggest each measure shows potential. Each of the assessments needs to be tested on the target population to evaluate the difficulty and discrimination capability of the measures specifically for the target population. Systems Thinking demonstrated appropriate discrimination in the pilot test; while some of the distractor response options may need to be altered for individual items to be most effective, if the Type 1 and Type 2 items are indeed reflecting a single Systems Thinking construct, there may be a sufficient number of strong items already and weaker items can simply be dropped. Problem Solver also demonstrated a strong ability to discriminate among participants. Although one item was recommended for deletion, there are a sufficient number of*

BODY-41   *"Future research is needed to examine the reliability and validity of the assessments within the target population of new Army officers. This includes evaluating convergent and discriminant validity, as well as criterion-related validity and exploring the capability of the measures to classify officers for various branch assignments."*

BODY-48   *"For this task, you are being asked to assign Soldiers to special units based on their qualifications. For each question you will be provided with the specific requirements for that special unit and a table of Soldiers from which to choose. You must examine the requirements for the special unit and then select the Soldiers that meet the requirements by double-clicking on their name in the table."*

BODY-49   *Over 200,000 square miles comprise the Caucasus, a mountainous region located between the Black Sea and the Caspian Sea. The Caucasus includes Atropia, Limaria, and Gorgas, as well as parts of Ariana and Donovia. The Caucasus Mountains, consisting of the Greater and Lesser Caucasus ranges, traditionally form the separation between Europe and Asia. The Caucasus region contains two major parts—the North Caucasus and the South.*

Research Note 2023-04

Development of Three Cognitive Assessments for Officer Classification

Chelsey Byrd
Personnel Decisions Research Institutes

Melissa Glorioso
U.S. Army Research Institute

Cory Adis
Lia Engelsted
Jacob Pfleger
Michelle Wisecarver
Personnel Decisions Research Institutes

January 2023

**United States Army Research Institute
for the Behavioral and Social Sciences**

U.S. Army Research Institute
for the Behavioral and Social Sciences

Department of the Army
Deputy Chief of Staff, G1

Authorized and approved:

MICHELLE L. ZBYLUT, Ph.D.
Director

Research accomplished under contract
for the Department of the Army by

Personnel Decisions Research Institutes

Technical review by

Dr. Krystal Roach, U.S. Army Research Institute

DISPOSITION

This Research Note has been submitted to the
Defense Technical Information Center (DTIC).

REPORT DOCUMENTATION PAGE

1. REPORT DATE (Month Year)	2. REPORT TYPE	3. DATES COVERED (Month Year)	
January 2023	Final	**START DATE** August 2021	**END DATE** June 2022

4. TITLE AND SUBTITLE

Development of Three Cognitive Assessments for Officer Classification

5a. CONTRACT NUMBER W911NF-20-C-0047	5b. GRANT NUMBER	5c. COOPERATIVE AGREEMENT NUMBER
5d. PROGRAM ELEMENT NUMBER 622785	**5e. PROJECT NUMBER** A790	**5f. TASK NUMBER** 1030 — **5g. WORK UNIT NUMBER**

6. AUTHOR(S)

Chelsey Byrd, Melissa Glorioso, Cory Adis, Lia Engelsted, Jacob Pfleger, Michelle Wisecarver

7. PERFORMING ORGANIZATION NAME(S) AND ADDRESS(ES)	8. PERFORMING ORGANIZATION REPORT NUMBER
Personnel Decisions Research Institutes 1911 N. Fort Myer Drive, Suite 410 Arlington, VA 22209	

9. SPONSORING/MONITORING AGENCY NAME(S) AND ADDRESS(ES)	10. SPONSOR/MONITOR'S ACRONYM(S)	11. SPONSOR/MONITOR'S REPORT NUMBER(S)
U.S. Army Research Institute for the Behavioral and Social Sciences 6000 6th Street (Bldg. 1464 / Mail Stop: 5610) Fort Belvoir, Virginia 22060-5610	ARI	Research Note 2023-04

12. DISTRIBUTION/AVAILABILITY STATEMENT

Distribution Statement A : Approved for public release; distribution unlimited.

13. SUPPLEMENTARY NOTES

ARI Research POC: Dr, Melissa Glorioso, Selection and Assignment Research Unit

14. ABSTRACT

Assessments, developed for the Army Research Institute for the Behavioral and Social Sciences, for three cognitive ability constructs identified in previous research as important for Army officers were assessed via a construct validity study and a pilot test study. Results from these studies were reviewed and it was found that the measures were generally functioning as intended, with all three assessments demonstrating the ability to differentiate between high and low performers. Testing procedures and specific findings for each construct are discussed.

15. SUBJECT TERMS

Officer cognitive ability, Officer assessment, Officer classification, Leadership, Systems Thinking, Problem solving, Multi-tasking

16. SECURITY CLASSIFICATION OF:			17. LIMITATION OF ABSTRACT	18. NUMBER OF PAGES
a. REPORT Unclassified	**b. ABSTRACT** Unclassified	**C. THIS PAGE** Unclassified	Unclassified Unlimited	53

19a. NAME OF RESPONSIBLE PERSON	19b. PHONE NUMBER (Include area code)
Dr. Tonia Heffner	(703)545-4408

Research Note 2023-04

Development of Three Cognitive Assessments for Officer Classification

Chelsey Byrd
Personnel Decisions Research Institutes

Melissa Glorioso
U.S. Army Research Institute

Cory Adis
Lia Engelsted
Jacob Pfleger
Michelle Wisecarver
Personnel Decisions Research Institutes

Selection and Assessment Research Unit
Tonia Heffner, Chief

January 2023

ACKNOWLEDGMENT

We would like to thank Jaclyn Martin, Gary Carter, Tracy Kantrowitz, and Drs. Jessica Carre and Karly Schleicher for their input on the development and reviews of items. We would also like to thank the ARI and PDRI personnel who completed the assessments for the pilot test and those who completed ratings for the construct validation analyses. Finally, we thank Dr. Krystal Roach for her suggestions and improvements on an earlier version of this report.

DEVELOPMENT OF THREE COGNITIVE ASSESSMENTS FOR OFFICER CLASSIFICATION

CONTENTS

APPENDICIES

LIST OF TABLES

CONTENTS (CONTINUED)

CONTENTS (CONTINUED)

LIST OF FIGURES

DEVELOPMENT OF THREE COGNITIVE ASSESSMENTS FOR OFFICER CLASSIFICATION

Introduction

Previous research by the U.S. Army Research Institute for the Behavioral and Social Sciences (ARI) researched possible measurement concepts for the assessment of 10 cognitive constructs important for officer performance (Wisecarver et al., in preparation): Analytic Thinking, Analyze Data or Information, Detail Focused and Precise, Processes Information and Data, Problem Solver, Perceptive, Multitasking, Systems Thinking, Interdisciplinary, and Technologically Adept. In that research, an initial set of possible assessment approaches for each construct was proposed and reviewed by a senior level ARI subject matter expert (SME) panel, generating a final recommended assessment approach and proof-of-concept items for six constructs. The review of the literature, proposed measurement concepts, and example items developed as part of the effort can be found in Wisecarver et al. (in preparation).

Three constructs were subsequently selected by ARI for the first phase of developing operational assessment tools: Systems Thinking, Problem Solver, and Multitasking. These constructs were chosen for further development because conceptually they were complementary to existing ARI measures and were deemed to be broadly applicable to officer success across multiple ranks and positions. Definitions for the three selected constructs can be seen in Table 1.

Table 1

Construct Definitions for Systems Thinking, Problem Solver, and Multitasking

Construct	Definition
Systems Thinking	Conceptualizes and understands relationships and arrangements within and between relevant components and structures
Problem Solver	Understands multiple approaches for representing and solving problems
Multitasking	The ability to shift attention between two or more tasks with minimal reduction in performance

The objective of this report is to describe the item and content development for these three constructs and initial results gathered regarding construct validity and descriptive characteristics of the items and scales. In the subsequent sections, the measure and item development approach for each of the three constructs is described in detail. The methods and results sections are then presented in a two-study format, describing first the construct validity study and then the pilot test of the three measures. A discussion and recommendations are provided for each construct.

Item Development

This section describes the measurement approach and item development process for each of the three constructs. Two of the constructs, Systems Thinking and Problem Solver, required developing a series of multiple-choice questions and response options. The third construct,

1

Multitasker, required developing the content of the assessment and a programming approach that would present the test taker with multiple tasks to complete. Throughout the development process, the construct definitions were used as a foundation to guide development decisions. Additional parameters that guided development included (a) only using content that did not require specific pre-existing knowledge, and (b) using language that reflected a grade level less than 12th grade, based on the Flesch-Kincaid Reading Level.

Systems Thinking

In the Systems Thinking measure, test takers demonstrate their understanding of the relationships and dynamics in systems by responding to a series of multiple-choice items that describe the relationships between or among elements of a system. For each item, the test taker needs to match a diagram representing a system to a text-based description of the system. Example items can be seen in Appendix A.

There are two types of items:

- Item Type 1: The test taker reads a text description of a system and selects the response option with the best graphical representation of the relationships in that system.
- Item Type 2: The test taker is presented with a graphic model or image of a system and asked to select the response option that best describes the graphical system using text.

System characteristics presented in the items are modeled after a variety of system types (i.e., biological, mechanical, social, etc.), but no knowledge of specific systems is required to respond to the items. Item content is a mix of fictitious and everyday topics. For each item type, an effort was made to develop a set of items that varied in difficulty level, although the actual difficulty level of the items will need to be established empirically. Key factors affecting item difficulty include the number of elements and the number and complexity of relationships in the system. With respect to number of elements, the systems presented in the items were designed to depict two to five elements to maintain an appropriate range of difficulty levels. With respect to relationships, simple relationships were designed by having multiple elements relate to only one other element in the system, while more complex relationships were designed by having elements relate to multiple other elements in the system.

Three item writers initially produced 12-15 items each, targeting a proportion of items to each of three levels - low, moderate, and high difficulty. Item writers were instructed to generate content that was general and broadly applicable to officers across all ranks and branches within the Army, avoiding content that would appear technical or scientific, as well as slang or informal jargon. Items were generally written to target a 9th-11th grade reading level. Each item was then subjected to at least five rounds of reviews from other project team members, making subsequent edits as needed. Following the rounds of reviews and edits, 37 items were selected to move forward for pilot testing: 18 Type 1 items and 19 Type 2 items.

Problem Solver

The Problem Solver measure is designed to assess the test taker's general problem-solving competence from two perspectives – whether they can (a) identify the best way to

2

approach a specific problem, and (b) determine the best way to represent a problem (see Table 1). These two aspects of problem solving were identified as key aspects of generalized, structured problem solving and selected as focal areas for the definition of Problem Solver (see Wisecarver et al., in preparation). A series of multiple-choice items were developed that use short, scenario-based stems to frame questions about the problems presented. The two types of items representing the two dimensions are as follows:

- *Approaches items:* Test takers are asked to identify the best approach for either solving or making progress toward solving a specific problem that is described in the item stem. Approaches items may also deal with formulating a plan based on chosen methods for solving a problem.
- *Representation items:* Test takers are asked to identify the best external representation of a problem given a problem-solving goal (e.g., reframing, communicating, understanding the problem).

The strategy used to develop items for Problem Solver was similar to that for Systems Thinking. Item writers were instructed to avoid domain-specific problems that would require technical or specialized knowledge, keep content general and broadly applicable to officers across all ranks and branches within the Army, avoid slang and jargon, and write items to target a 9th-11th grade reading level. Because the Problem Solver construct captures understanding multiple approaches for representing and solving problems, the items were designed to capture a broad base of approaches and representations, making them more formative than reflective.

Five developers produced three to 10 items each, for a total of 38 initial items: 18 Approaches items and 20 Representation items. Each item was then subjected to at least five rounds of reviews and subsequent edits. While correct responses for Representation items were based on prescriptions in the literature for creating external representations and visualizations in problem-solving, correct responses for Approaches items were determined based on SME ratings. To determine the correct responses, five subject matter experts (SMEs) with experience assessing problem solving and a MA or PhD in I/O Psychology, independently identified the best responses for each Approaches item. Initial ratings showed 100% agreement for two out of 18 items. Raters then engaged in consensus discussions regarding the remaining 16 items. The consensus discussions centered on identifying aspects of the item content that could be modified in order to make the best approach unambiguous. Following item content modifications, the remaining items achieved 100% agreement among the five raters regarding the best response.

After the multiple rounds of reviews and modifications, 36 items measuring the two dimensions (18 Approaches items and 18 Representation items) moved forward for pilot testing. Example items can be seen in Appendix B.

Multitasking

The concept for the Multitasking measure was to create a dual task measure that consisted of a primary visual search task and a secondary interruption task. Unlike Systems Thinking and Problem Solver, the Multitasking construct is not conducive to measurement with multiple-choice questions and responses. The Multitasking measure needed to capture a test taker's ability to engage in time-sharing and task shifting. While many types of content could have been used for the time-sharing and task shifting tasks, the decision was made to use content specifically relevant to the Army; this contextualization provided an Army character to the tasks,

3

yet they did not require any specific Army knowledge to complete them. Parameters for developing the assessment included having tasks that were low in complexity, avoid mathematical and technical content, and have minimal requirements for computer resources. With these objectives and parameters in mind, PDRI developed a computer-based Multitasking measure consisting of a primary and a distractor task. This requires the test taker to engage in attention switching in order to complete both tasks within the same time period.

Multiple concepts were considered for both the primary and distractor tasks. The tasks needed to be detailed enough that the test taker would have to concentrate and focus in order to answer the questions about the content correctly, but simple enough that each item could be completed rather quickly. Another major consideration was to ensure the distractor task was sufficiently different from the primary task that it would require the test taker to mentally "switch" between tasks. The goal was to have the content differ enough that it would distract the test taker and therefore affect their performance on the primary task as they mentally switched between the primary and distractor tasks. The identification and refinement of the two tasks and their content was iterative, with the development team engaging in multiple sessions to review possible tasks and content areas and to determine the extent to which different measurement strategies met the criteria needed for the two tasks.

The two tasks that were selected for development include a primary task that requires the test taker to identify whether fictitious Soldiers meet a set of selection criteria, and an interruption task that requires the test taker to proofread lines of text. The primary task presents the test taker with a list of Soldiers, which includes their name, career field, rank, time in grade, and whether they are currently deployable. The test taker is asked to indicate whether each Soldier meets a specific set of qualifications so that they can be assigned to a special unit. The test taker must provide these decisions within a specified amount of time, or else the question is marked as incorrect and the test progresses to the next question. To prevent test takers from memorizing the lists or qualifications, new criteria and Soldiers with different qualifications were used for each new block of the test. Ultimately, 12 blocks of primary task questions and content were developed, with each block containing eight items, for a total of 96 items. After an initial set of uninterrupted calibration items, each block was separated by an interruption task. The average time to complete the five calibration items was used to determine the length of time a test taker would be given to complete the primary task questions. After completing those items, test takers were routed to one of 10 pre-programed tests configured to time limits ranging from five to 14 seconds. The time limit obtained on the calibration items was used throughout the rest of the primary task blocks of the test. The purpose of this was to establish the test taker's standard pace for the task so that the task was sufficiently difficult for each test taker despite natural differences in reaction and processing times.

The interruption task asks the test taker to review lines of text to identify any duplicate words (i.e., words repeated in error). Thus, the interruption task does not actually require reading comprehension of the text or knowledge regarding spelling or grammar; rather, the test taker needs to scan the lines of text to identify any repeated words. The test taker is asked to identify each line of text that has an error by checking a box next to that line. The amount of time a test taker is given to complete the interruption task is not constrained; this is because the intention is to have all test takers switch their focus to the interruption task and spend the time needed to complete the task correctly, regardless of how long it takes them. The interruption task therefore remains on the screen until the test taker clicks "Next" to continue with the Soldier identification task. At that time, the next set of primary task items appear, and the cycle of primary task and interruption task is repeated. Text for the interruption task was taken from the Army's Decisive Action Training Content (U.S. Army TRADOC G-2, 2019). Example content from the primary and interruption tasks can be seen in Appendix C.

Scoring of the Multitasking measure focuses on comparing an individual's base task score without interruptions to their base task score with interruptions. Because the Multitasking measure is a new measure, it was considered appropriate to empirically test more than one scoring approach in order to identify the scoring approach that would produce the strongest descriptive properties. One scoring approach compares performance on the initial block of primary task questions before the interruption task is introduced with performance on later primary task blocks that are separated by interruption tasks. The other approach examines differences in item-level performance, allowing for comparison of the participant's accuracy when it is not impacted by the distractor task with accuracy when it has been recently impacted by the distractor task.

Evaluation Approach

Each of the three construct measures that was developed was then examined in two preliminary evaluation studies. The first study sought to evaluate the construct validity of the measures using SME ratings, and the second study examined preliminary descriptive statistics for each measure using a small pilot test sample.

Study 1

An initial study was conducted to evaluate the construct validity of the three measures using assessment SMEs.

Method

Seven assessment SMEs who were not involved with the development of the measures, participated in the construct validity rating study. Six had PhDs in I/O Psychology and one had a PhD in Experimental Psychology with a focus on I/O Psychology. Participants' levels of experience included two who recently completed their PhD, two with 1-2 years of experience beyond graduate school, and three who had five or more years of experience beyond graduate school. The amount of time participants reported working for their current employer ranged from seven months to 23 and a half years, with a mean of six and a half years.

Participants were provided with general instructions for completing the construct validity rating task and a general description of the officer cognitive measures. For each of the three measures, participants were also provided with specific rating instructions, a construct definition, a description of the measure and scoring strategy for that construct, and example items. Rating instructions asked participants to indicate the extent to which the measurement strategy represented an appropriate way to measure the whole construct based on the definition provided.

Raters used the following scale: 1 = is not an appropriate way to measure the whole construct, 2 = is a somewhat appropriate way to measure the whole construct, and 3 = is a very appropriate way to measure the whole construct. If participants selected a response of one or

5

two, they were asked to make a second rating for the measurement strategy, indicating the extent to which the measurement strategy represented an appropriate way to measure part of the construct based on the definition provided. The same rating scale was used for the follow up question with a modification of the term "whole construct" to "part of the construct."

Results

Systems Thinking

Six of the seven SMEs rated the Systems Thinking measure a "3," indicating that the proposed measurement approach for Systems Thinking was a very appropriate way to measure the whole construct. One SME rated the proposed measurement approach as a somewhat appropriate way (rating = "2") to measure the whole construct and a very appropriate way to measure part of the construct (rating = "3"). In the comments section, this SME indicated that they found the measure to be a very appropriate way to specifically measure the aspect of systems thinking that involves understanding system dynamics.

Problem Solver

Results for Problem Solver indicated that four SMEs rated the proposed measure a "3," indicating it was a very appropriate way to measure the whole construct. The other three SMEs indicated that the proposed measure was only a somewhat appropriate way to measure the whole construct (rating = "2"). Raters provided a number of comments, which can be seen in Table 2.

Of the three SMEs that rated the measurement strategy as a somewhat appropriate way to measure the whole construct (rating = "2"), two rated the proposed measurement approach as a very appropriate way to measure *part* of the construct (rating = "3"). One of these SMEs expressed concern that the multiple-choice format of the response options may not allow for participants to form their own external representations (see Topic 1 in Table 2). The other SME highlighted a mismatch between the "Approaches" definition, which describes "identifying methods..." for solving a problem, and the measure, which asks participants to "identify the best approach" for solving a problem (see Topic 3 in Table 2).

Finally, one SME rated the proposed measurement approach as a somewhat appropriate way (rating = "2") to measure both the whole construct and part of the construct. This was the lowest rating given in the study, although still an acceptable rating for the measure. In providing an explanation for the rating, the SME expressed a general concern that the items and response options were too vague. The SME also expressed specific concerns regarding the appropriateness of the "Approaches" response options, indicating that some seemed too broad, and some seemed like better ways to represent a problem than to approach and solve it (see Topic 2 in Table 2).

6

Table 2

Problem Solver Construct Validity SME Comments

Topic	Comment
1. Representations Subdimension	The "representations" subdimension specifically identifies skill in forming external representations, but the items seem to ask about knowledge of the best ways, instead of specifically testing the ability to "form" external representations. The multiple-choice format does not lend itself to an individual creating something externally. However, participants may be internally "forming" external representations and then picking the item that most closely represents what they thought of after reading the item stem.
2. General & Approaches Subdimension	The items and options are a bit vague.
	Also, it seems like any of the approaches listed would be subsumed under the response option "working backward from the goal to determine the issue." Other response options provided seem like ways to represent (versus solve) a problem (e.g., "think of an analogy or metaphor for the problem" and "leave the problem alone for a while, then come back to it later").
3. Approaches Subdimension	I think the "representation" items are appropriate from a construct measurement perspective, but I had a minor concern with the "approaches" items. I recognize the benefits of using multiple choice formats for this assessment but providing several options for "approaches" doesn't seem to converge with the construct definition of "identifying methods..." (as opposed to identifying the "best" method). It almost seems as if the item format is providing "answers."
4. Scoring	Since the prompt says, "All the following approaches are valid ways to solve a problem, but which one would work best in this situation?" an alternative scoring method would be to assign points to response options, giving more points to more desirable responses and fewer points to less desirable responses.

Multitasking

Results indicated that five of the seven SMEs rated the proposed measures for Multitasking as a "3," or a very appropriate way to measure the whole construct. The other two SMEs rated the proposed measurement approach as a somewhat appropriate way to measure the whole construct (rating = "2") and a very appropriate way to measure part of the construct (rating = "3"). One of these two SMEs expressed concern that the time constraint aspect of the measure may impact the validity of the scores (see Topic 1 in Table 3). The other SME expressed concern regarding two issues: a) a need for more clarification regarding the scoring procedure to ensure scores would be comparable across different samples, and b) that the two measures of reading and searching for information may not be the most effective way to measure attention shifting (see Topic 2 in Table 3). All rater comments concerning Multitasking can be seen in Table 3.

Table 3

Multitasking Construct Validity SME Comments

Topic	Comment
1. Scoring	Timing the measure may impact validity of your Multitasking scores. From my understanding, tests that incorporate time constraints are useful to measure cognitive ability, but might increase test taker anxiety, result in negative test perceptions, increase guessing, etc., thereby resulting in questionable construct validity.
2. Scoring, Attention Shifting	Related to the measurement, is a "minimal reduction in performance" a standardized number? Will participants score higher if they are closer to the "minimal" number identified, or be ranked from least to greatest reduction in performance? In the next administration of this test, the sample may differ greatly, and without a benchmark for what "minimal reduction" means, scores between different populations will not be equivalent. Also, both tasks involve reading and searching for information, so I wonder how much attention shifting the participant is really engaging in.
3. Measurement Tasks	It seems like there could be many of different definitions of multi-tasking and one difference between them might be whether the two tasks are discrete or overlapping. This measure includes two discrete tasks and it aligns with the construct definition, but it would also be possible to measure overlapping tasks while aligning with the construct definition, resulting in a measure that looked very different.
4. Measurement Tasks	I had to read the measurement description a few times to fully understand it. Initially I was concerned that segmenting the two different tasks was not the best approach to mimic Multitasking, but I think the proposed scoring mechanism makes the assessment appropriate for this construct.

Study 2

A pilot test of the three measures was conducted using a small number of participants to collect initial descriptive data on the measures. This included measures such as the distribution of scores, item difficulties, distractor response option performance, and item-total correlations where relevant.

Method

The pilot test was completed by a convenience sample of 19 volunteers from ARI and PDRI. Eleven participants were female and eight were male. Participants ranged in age from 24-63 years, with a mean age of 32 years. One participant identified as Hispanic or Latino. Sixteen participants identified as White, and one each identified as American Indian or Alaska Native,

Asian, and Black. All participants had post high school education, with seven reporting a BA degree and twelve reporting a MA or PhD.

Participants were provided with general instructions for completing the pilot test and links to access the three individual assessments. Detailed instructions for completing each assessment were located within the assessments. Participants were asked to ensure they had ample time to complete each assessment uninterrupted within the estimated time to complete each assessment (20-40 minutes depending on the assessment). Participants were also advised to take a break between assessments as each assessment would require focused cognitive engagement. Each participant was provided with a unique participant identification number and asked to enter this number during each assessment so that the data from each of the three assessments could be linked.

Results

All 19 participants completed each of the three measures and there was no missing or unusable data for any of the participants. Results for each construct are described in the following sections, including summaries of overall and subdimension scale scores as well as response option performance.

Systems Thinking

There were seven items that all participants answered correctly. These items were not included in the calculation of scale scores. Scores on the Systems Thinking scale ranged from 37% to 97% with a distribution that was slightly negatively skewed (see Figure 1). Twenty-five percent of participants scored below 70%, while 74% of participants scored 70% or higher, with most of those scoring 80% or higher. The mean score was 75% with a standard deviation of 19%. The percentage of participants in each score range can be seen in Table 4.

Figure 1

Overall Systems Thinking Scale Score Histogram

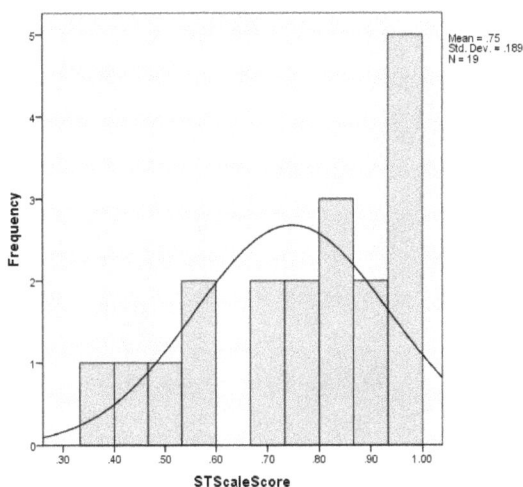

Table 4

Overall Systems Thinking Scale Scores

Score Range	Number of Participants	Percent of Total Participants	Summary Percentages
30%-39%	1	5%	
40%-49%	1	5%	Scores below 70%
50%-59%	3	16%	25%
60%-69%	0	0%	
70%-79%	4	21%	
80%-89%	5	26%	Scores of 70% and higher
90%-97%	5	26%	74%

Note. The combined total percent is equal to 99% due to rounding.

When examining scores on the two different item types, results showed that participants performed similarly on Type 1 and Type 2 items, with scale scores distributed across each item type's respective range (see Figures 2 and 3). When separating items by type, scale scores ranged from 33% to 100% for Type 1 items and from 40% to 100% for Type 2 items (see Tables 5 and 6). Mean scores were 75% with a standard deviation of 24% for Type 1 items and 75% with a standard deviation of 16% for Type 2 items. The number of participants in each score range for Type 1 and Type 2 items can be seen in Tables 5 and 6.

Figure 2

Systems Thinking Type 1 Scale Scores Histogram

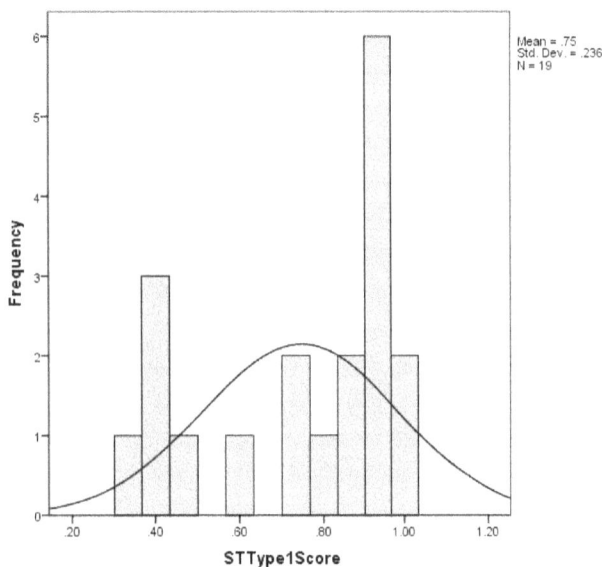

Figure 3

Systems Thinking Type 2 Scale Scores Histogram

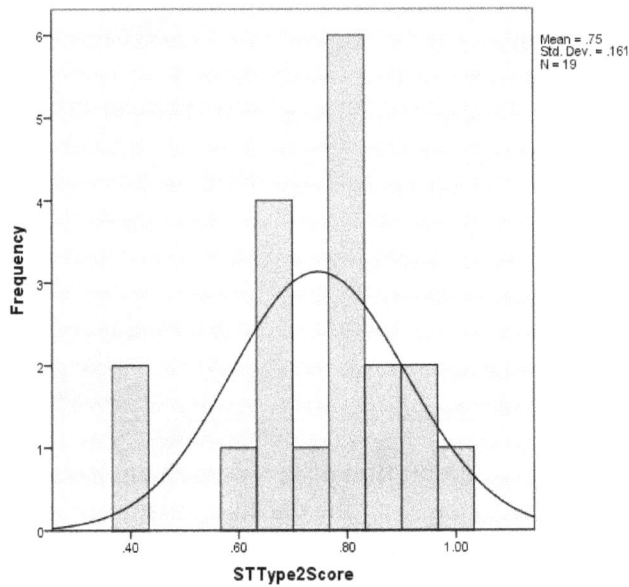

Table 5

Systems Thinking Type 1 Scale Scores

Score Range	Number of Participants	Percent of Total Participants	Summary Percentages
33%-39%	1	5%	
44%-49%	4	21%	Scores below 70%
50%-59%	0	0%	31%
60%-69%	1	5%	
70%-79%	2	11%	
80%-89%	3	16%	Scores of 70% and higher
90%-100%	8	42%	69%

Table 6

Systems Thinking Type 2 Scale Scores

Score Range	Number of Participants	Percent of Total Participants	Summary Percentages
40%-49%	2	11%	
50%-59%	0	0%	Scores below 70%
60%-69%	5	26%	37%
70%-79%	1	5%	
80%-89%	8	42%	Scores of 70% and higher
90%-100%	3	16%	84%

Item difficulties were calculated by examining the proportion of people who answered each question correctly out of the total number of people answering the question; that is, items for which fewer people answered correctly are considered to be more difficult. Results indicated that there were 10 very easy items (27%), which were answered correctly by 90-100% of the participants, and nine additional items (24%) that were answered correctly by 80-89% of participants. Only a small percentage of items were very high in difficulty, with three items (8%) that were answered correctly by fewer than half of participants. Four of the five most difficult items, which were answered correctly by 13% or fewer of participants, were all Type 2 items. The distribution of item difficulties can be seen in Table 7.

Table 7

Systems Thinking Item Difficulties

Percentage Answering Correctly	Number of Items (Total)	Type 1 Items	Type 2 Items	Percent of Items (Total)
40%-49%	3	0	3	8%
50%-59%	2	1	1	5%
60%-69%	4	4	0	11%
70%-79%	9	6	3	24%
80%-89%	9	4	5	24%
90%-100%	10	3	7	27%

Note. The Percent of Items (Total) column sums to 99% due to rounding.

In general, the distractor response options seemed to offer participants reasonable alternative responses. There were seven items (19%) that were answered correctly by all participants; thus, for these items none of the distractors were selected. For 14 of the items (38%), only one distractor response option was selected in addition to the correct response. For the other 16 items, either two or all three other distractor response options were selected. The distribution of the number of distractors selected was similar for both Type 1 and Type 2 items. The distributions of the distractor response option selection can be seen in Table 8.

Table 8

Systems Thinking Distractor Response Option Performance

Number of Distractors Selected	Number of Items (Total)	Type 1 Items	Type 2 Items	Percent of Items (Total)
0	7	3	4	19%
1	14	7	7	38%
2	11	5	6	30%
3	5	3	2	14%

Note. The Percent of Items (Total) column sums to 101% due to rounding.

With a pilot test sample size of only 19, it was not possible to calculate the internal consistency of the Systems Thinking scale, however, item total correlations were calculated by examining the correlation of each item to the scale calculated without that individual item. Before calculating item total correlations, the seven items with no variance were removed. Of the 30 items examined, 15 demonstrated item total correlations of .50 or higher with the overall Systems Thinking score, which included 10 Type 1 items and five Type 2 items. Of the remaining items, 10 demonstrated correlations with the overall Systems Thinking score of .00 to .50, and four were negatively correlated with the overall score (see Table 9).

When examining the correlations between items and subscale scores, it was found that nine Type 1 items demonstrated item total correlations of .50 or greater with the Type 1 scale score. Of the remaining Type 1 items, five demonstrated correlations between .00 and .49 and one demonstrated a negative correlation. Results were similar for the Type 2 items, with five items demonstrating a correlation of .50 or greater, seven demonstrating a correlation of .00 to .49, and three items demonstrating a negative correlation (see Table 9).

Specific correlations for all 30 items that were examined in this portion of the data analysis can be seen in Table 9. Results were also combined into tables that summarize the performance of all 37 items by type (see Appendix D, Tables D1 and D2).

13

Table 9

Systems Thinking Items with Item Total Correlations

Item	Correlation with Overall Score	Correlation with Type 1 Score	Correlation with Type 2 Score
	Type 1 Items		
ST 1	.53	.38	--
ST 2	.41	.44	--
ST 3	.65	.58	--
ST 5	.13	.08	--
ST 7	-.03	-.07	--
ST 8	.53	.55	--
ST 9	.60	.66	--
ST 10	.44	.43	--
ST 11	.55	.59	--
ST 12	.65	.50	--
ST 13	.13	.13	--
ST 14	.52	.51	--
ST 15	.75	.75	--
ST 17	.58	.63	--
ST 18	.54	.54	--
	Type 2 Items		
ST 19	-.36	--	-.28
ST 20	.56	--	.62
ST 21	.21	--	.02
ST 22	.02	--	.03
ST 23	-.26	--	-.23
ST 26	.75	--	.53
ST 27	.66	--	.50
ST 28	-.15	--	-.17
ST 29	.39	--	.35

14

Table 9, continued

	Type 2 Items (continued)		
ST 31	.48	--	.41
ST 32	.40	--	.27
ST 33	.18	--	.15
ST 34	.65	--	.70
ST 35	.41	--	.45
ST 36	.71	--	.62

Notes. Items 1-18 are Type 1 and items 19-37 are Type 2. Seven items with no variance were excluded.

Problem Solver

Scale scores were calculated for an Overall Problem Solver scale as well as Approaches and Representation scales. When calculating scale scores, two items that all participants answered incorrectly (one Approaches and one Representation item) and two items that all participants answered correctly (two Approaches items) were removed, for a total of 32 items included in the scale analyses out of the original 36 items. Overall Problem Solver scores ranged from 44% to 66% with a distribution that was truncated at the tails but approximately normal (see Figure 4). The majority of participants scored in the middle score bracket (50-59%), with 63% receiving a score within this range (see Table 10).

Figure 4

Overall Problem Solver Scale Scores Histogram

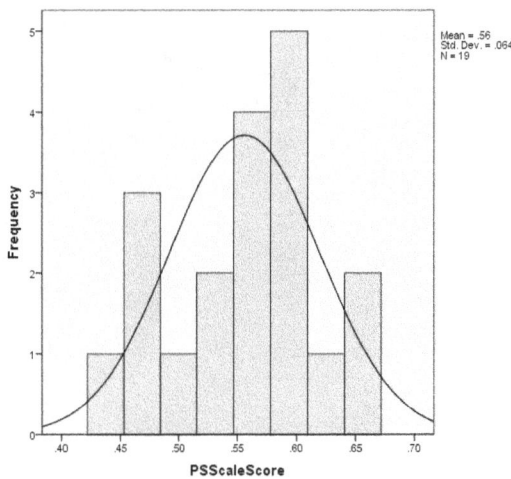

15

Table 10

Overall Problem Solver Scale Scores

Score Range	Number of Participants	Percent of Total Participants
44%-49%	4	21%
50%-59%	12	63%
60%-64%	3	15%

Note. Total is equal to 99% due to rounding.

Participants performed more poorly on Approaches items than they did on Representation items. Scores ranged from 40% to 67% on the Approaches subscale and from 38% to 81% on the Representation subscale. Mean subdimension scores were 52% (*SD* = 7%) for Approaches, and 63% (*SD* = 10%) for Representations. Both subdimensions appeared to be difficult, resulting in low participant scores and a therefore a restricted range. However, scores were normally distributed within their respective ranges (see Figures 5 and 6). The distribution of participant scores for the Approaches and Representation subdimensions can be seen in Tables 11 and 12, respectively.

Figure 5

Problem Solver Approaches Scale Scores Histogram

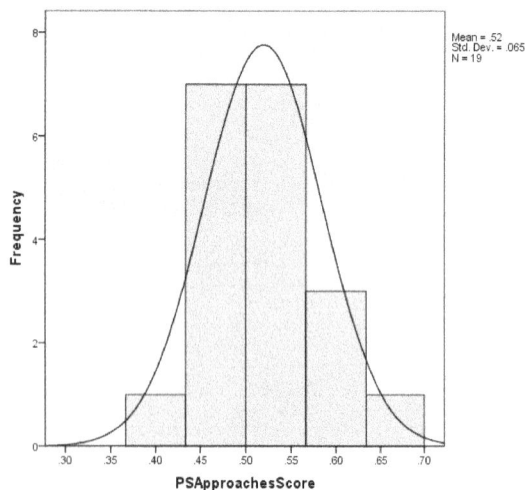

Figure 6

Problem Solver Representation Scale Scores Histogram

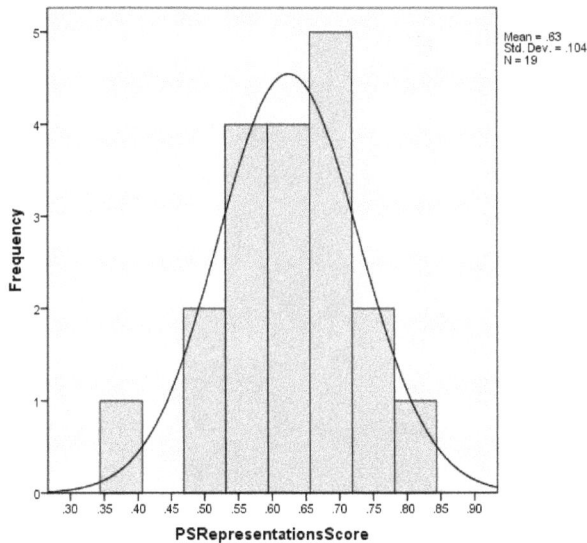

Table 11

Problem Solver Approaches Scale Scores

Score Range	Number of Participants	Percent of Total Participants
44%-49%	8	42%
50%-59%	7	37%
60%-69%	4	21%

Item difficulties were calculated by examining the proportion of people who answered the question correctly out of the total number of people answering the question. Results indicated that participants generally found the items to be difficult with 41% of items being answered correctly by less than half of participants. There were twice as many Approaches items (10) as Representations items (5) within this low scoring category. However, within the displayed range of item difficulties there was an even distribution of scores, with items both at the top and bottom of the distribution for which all or nearly all participants answered correctly (at the high end of the range) or incorrectly (at the low end of the range). The distribution of item difficulties can be seen in Table 13.

17

Table 12

Problem Solver Representation Scale Scores

Score Range	Number of Participants	Percent of Total Participants
30%-39%	1	5%
40%-49%	0	0%
50%-59%	6	32%
60%-69%	9	47%
70%-79%	2	11%
80%-89%	1	5%

Table 13

Problem Solver Item Difficulties

Percentage Answering Correctly	Number of Items (Total)	Approaches Items	Representations Items	Percent of Items (Total)	Summary Percentage
0%-9%	3	2	1	8%	
10%-19%	2	0	2	6%	
20%-29%	3	2	1	8%	41%
30%-39%	3	2	1	8%	
40%-49%	4	4	0	11%	
50%-59%	2	0	2	6%	
60%-69%	7	2	5	19%	
70%-79%	5	1	4	14%	59%
80%-89%	5	3	2	14%	
90%-100%	2	2	0	6%	

In general, the Problem Solver distractor response options were reasonably appealing to participants. The distribution of the number of distractors selected was negatively skewed, with participants selecting none of the distractors provided for only two of the items, and all three distractors for 10 of the items (see Table 14). For one item (Item 3), 17 participants selected the same distractor option, two participants each selected one of the other two distractor options, and zero participants selected the correct option. In total, there were four items (Items 3, 5, 23, and 34) that demonstrated this pattern, in which one response option dominated and few or no

18

participants responded to the item correctly. Two of these items were Approaches items and two were Representation items. Across all items, at least one of the distractors was selected for 95% of questions, and all three distractors within a question were selected for 28% of questions.

Table 14

Problem Solver Distractor Response Option Performance

Number of Distractors Selected	Number of Items (Total)	Approaches Items	Representations Items	Percent of Total Items (Total)
0	2	2	0	6%
1	10	6	4	28%
2	14	6	8	39%
3	10	4	6	28%

Note. Percent of Total Items column sums to 101% due to rounding.

Although the Problem Solver construct was expected to be more formative in nature than reflective, item total correlations were calculated using data from the 19 participants by examining the correlation of each item to the scale calculated without that individual item. Before calculating item total correlations, the four items with no variance were removed.

The item-total correlations, particularly for Approaches, were largely in the negative direction. Few correlations reached statistical significance, reflecting the formative nature of the construct as well as the very small sample size. Approaches items showed 12 negatively signed and 3 positively signed correlations with the Overall Problem Solver score and Representation items showed 10 negative and 7 positive correlations (see Table 15). The magnitude of the item total correlations tended to be small to moderate (correlations of magnitude smaller than +/- .456 are nonsignificant). When examining item total correlations with the subscale scores, only one Approaches item was positively correlated with the Approaches subscale score, and 10 Representation items were positively correlated with the Representations subscale score. A summary of results for each of the 36 Problem Solver items can be seen in Appendix D (see Tables D3 and D4).

19

Table 15

Problem Solver Item Total Correlations

Item	Overall Score Correlation	Approaches Correlation	Representation Correlation
Approaches Items			
PS 1	-.22	-.43	--
PS 2	-.10	-.31	--
PS 4	-.43	-.51	--
PS 5	-.21	-.18	--
PS 6	.38	-.12	--
PS 8	-.19	-.21	--
PS 9	-.49	-.28	--
PS 10	-.27	-.04	--
PS 11	-.05	-.22	--
PS 12	-.09	-.40	--
PS 13	-.19	-.37	--
PS 14	-.11	-.23	--
PS 15	.19	.29	--
PS 16	.12	-.47	--
PS 17	-.44	-.63	--
Representations Items			
PS 19	.58	--	.60
PS 20	.28	--	.25
PS 21	-.23	--	-.29
PS 22	-.25	--	-.09
PS 23	-.12	--	-.19
PS 24	-.40	--	-.51
PS 25	.22	--	.14

Table 15, continued

Item	Overall Score Correlation	Approaches Correlation	Representation Correlation
PS 26	-.07	--	.03
PS 27	.14	--	.07
PS 28	.43	--	.27
PS 29	-.31	--	-.29
PS 31	-.27	--	-.38
PS 32	.18	--	.12
PS 33	.38	--	.19
PS 34	-.03	--	.02
PS 35	-.21	--	.04
PS 36	-.39	--	-.45

Note. Items 1-18 are Approaches and items 19-36 are Representation. Items with no variance were removed.

Multitasking

Participants generally performed well on both the Primary and Distractor tasks for this measure. At the start of the assessment, the program determines a calibration time for each participant that reflects their average response time. The goal of the calibration function is to identify an appropriate pace for each participant that is neither too difficult nor too easy to accomplish the tasks. Calibration response times ranged from 5-11 seconds with a standard deviation of 1.6 seconds. Based on their initial responses, 74% of participants were calibrated to a time of seven seconds or less per question. The percentage of participants within each range of calibration times can be seen in Table 16.

Table 16

Multitasking Calibration Times

Seconds	Number of Participants	Percent of Total Participants	Summary Percentages
5	3	16%	
6	6	32%	74%
7	5	26%	
8	2	11%	
9	2	11%	
10	0	0%	27%
11	1	5%	

Note. Total sum of each percentage column is equal to 101% due to rounding.

In general, participants answered the Primary task items correctly; all participants selected the correct response option for 63 out of 96 items. There were 33 items for which one or more participant answered incorrectly. There were also 20 items for which one or more participants provided no response, presumably because they were not quick enough to select a response.

Primary task scale scores were calculated as an average of participants' scores on all the items within the Primary Multitasking assessment. Overall Primary task scale scores ranged from 78% to 95% with a normal distribution, although reflecting a range that was restricted at the low end (see Figure 7). The majority of participants (53%) scored in the 86-90% range. The percentage of participants within each range of scale scores can be seen in Table 17.

22

Figure 7

Multitasking Primary Task Scale Scores Histogram

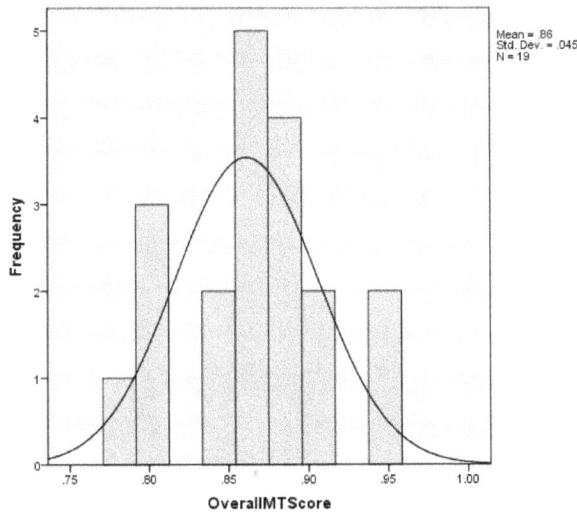

Table 17

Multitasking Primary Task Scale Scores

Score Range	Number of Participants	Percent of Total Participants
78%-80%	4	21%
81%-85%	3	16%
86%-90%	10	53%
91%-95%	2	11%

Note. Percent total is equal to 101% due to rounding.

Distractor task scale scores were calculated as an average of two sub-scores: (a) the percent of correct responses selected (i.e., lines of text with duplicate words correctly selected by the participant), and (b) the percent of incorrect responses ignored (lines of text without duplicate words not marked by the participant). Overall Distractor scale scores ranged from 77% to 100% with a mean of 91% and a standard deviation of 6%. The majority of participants scored in the high end of the displayed range, with 85% (32% + 21% + 32%) receiving a score of 85%-100%. Within this range the distribution of scores was normal (see Figure 8). The percentage of participants within each range of scores can be seen in Table 18.

Figure 8

Multitasking Distractor Scale Scores Histogram

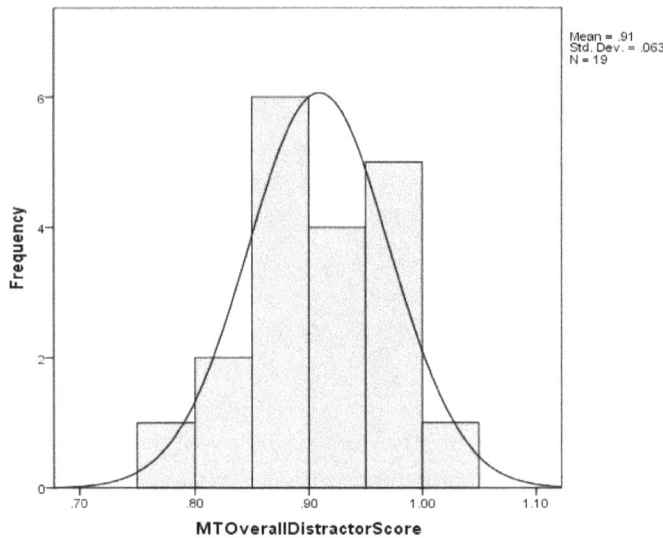

Table 18

Multitasking Distractor Scale Scores

Score Range	Number of Participants	Percent of Total Participants
77%-79%	1	5%
80%-84%	2	11%
85%-89%	6	32%
90%-94%	4	21%
95%-100%	6	32%

Note. Percent total is equal to 101% due to rounding.

Actual scores on the Multitasking scale were calculated by considering the decrement in performance caused by having the Distractor task interrupt the Primary task. Performance decrement was calculated in two ways: first by examining the difference between performance in the initial trial where participants completed the Primary task without interruptions and the subsequent trials which included the Distractor task. Results based on this scoring approach indicated that the assessment was working as designed, with 73% of participants showing a 10%-20% decrement in performance on the Primary task with the addition of the Distractor task. Using this approach, the distribution was positively skewed (see Figure 9). The percentage of participants within each range of scores using this first scoring approach can be seen in Table 19.

Figure 9

Multitasking Performance Decrement Scale Scores - First Approach Histogram

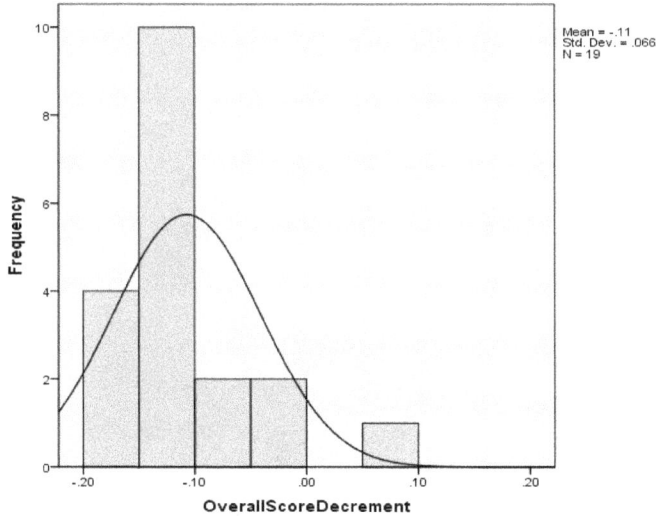

Table 19

Multitasking Performance Decrement Scale Scores - First Approach

Score Range	Number of Participants	Percent of Total Participants
-20% to -15%	5	26%
-14% to -10%	9	47%
-9% to -5%	2	11%
-4% to 0%	2	11%
1% to 6%	1	5%

In the second scoring approach used to calculate performance decrement, the subject's accuracy on the two items preceding each Distractor task was compared to their accuracy on the two items following each Distractor task. The average of the difference in performance was then calculated. This scoring approach resulted in almost half of participants (48%) demonstrating a 1%-15% increase in performance, and only 10% of participants demonstrating a 10%-20% performance decrement. Most of the remaining scores (42%) showed either no change (5 scores or 26% with 0% change) or a slight decrease in performance (3 scores or 16% with a 1-4% decrease). The distribution of participant scores within the observed range was normal (see Figure 10). The percentage of participants within each range of scores using this second scoring approach can be seen in Table 20.

Figure 10

Multitasking Performance Decrement Scale Scores - Second Approach

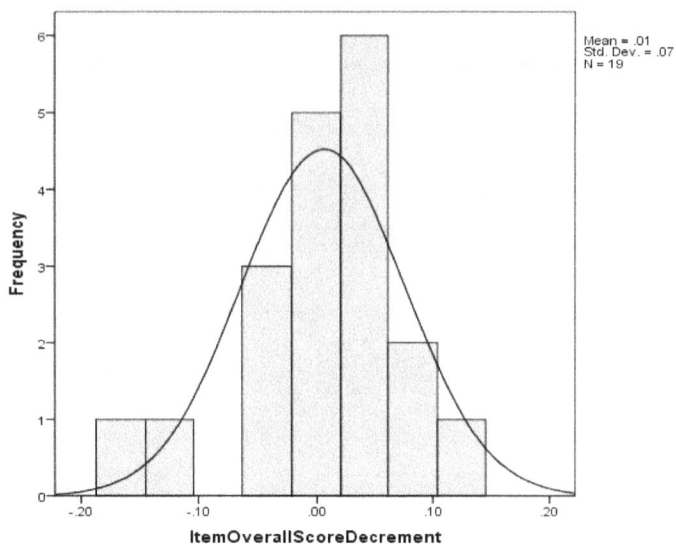

Table 20

Multitasking Performance Decrement Scale Scores - Second Approach

Score Range	Number of Participants	Percent of Total Participants
-20% to -15%	1	5%
-14% to -10%	1	5%
-9% to -5%	0	0%
-4% to 0%	8	42%
1% to 5%	6	32%
6% to 10%	2	11%
11% to 15%	1	5%

26

Construct Interrelationships

Correlations among the three constructs were examined, using both the overall and dimensional scores for Systems Thinking and Problem Solving, and using the Multitasking First Approach calculation (see Table 21). The correlation between the two Systems Thinking scales was significant and very high ($r = .81$, $p < .01$) and the correlation between the two Problem Solver dimensions was very low and not significant ($r = .14$, ns). The Overall Systems Thinking scale was significantly correlated with Overall Problem Solver ($r = .61$, $p < .01$) and Multitasking ($r = .57$, $p < .05$), although Overall Problem Solver and Multitasking were not significantly correlated ($r = .40$, ns). Overall Systems Thinking and Systems Thinking Type 1 were significantly correlated with Problem Solving Representation ($r = .52$, $p < .05$; $r = .56$ $p < .05$), but not Problem Solving Approaches ($r = .14$, *n.s.*). Multitasking was significantly correlated with all three Systems Thinking scales scores but not significantly correlated with any of the Problem Solver scales.

Table 21

Officer Cognitive Ability Scale Score Correlation Matrix

	ST Overall Scale	ST Type 1	ST Type 2	PS Overall Scale	PS Approaches	PS Represen-tation	Multi-tasking
ST Overall Scale	--						
ST Type 1	.97**	--					
ST Type 2	.93**	.81**	--				
PS Overall Scale	.61**	.63**	.50*	--			
PS Approaches	.39	.37	.37	.59**	--		
PS Representation	.52*	.56*	.40	.88**	.14	--	
Multitasking	.57*	.54*	.54*	.40	.22	.36	--

** Correlation is significant at the 0.01 level (2-tailed).
* Correlation is significant at the 0.05 level (2-tailed).

Discussion

Operational measures were developed for three cognitive ability constructs previously identified as important for officers: Systems Thinking, Problem Solver, and Multitasking. The newly-developed measures were then reviewed to determine whether they were functioning as intended. SME ratings collected in Study 1 generally supported the overall construct validity of the measures, and preliminary pilot test data collected in Study 2 showed that the measures had a reasonable ability to discriminate among participants. Specific findings and recommendations regarding each construct will be discussed.

Systems Thinking

SME ratings provided strong support for the construct validity of the Systems Thinking measurement approach. Only one SME rated the measurement approach as "somewhat" appropriate rather than "very" appropriate. This person indicated that they thought the measure specifically captured the understanding system dynamics aspect of systems thinking rather than the entire construct. Systems Thinking is a highly complex cognitive skill that has many knowledge and skill components. With the current measure we were specifically striving to capture whether individuals could *conceptualize and understand relationships and arrangements within and between relevant components and structures.* Given that there are infinite types of relationships that can occur within and between components, it would be impractical to try to measure an individual's ability to understand them all. The idea with the current measure is to use dynamic relationships to test individuals' understanding of relationships and arrangements because they represent a reasonable exemplar of relationships that might be encountered in complex systems. Although there are other types of relationships that could be tested, this content seemed to most SMEs to be a reasonable method to test individuals' general capability to understand relationships and arrangements within and between relevant components and structures. Given this, no changes are recommended for the Systems Thinking measure based on the results of Study 1.

In the second study, scores for Systems Thinking were generally 70% or higher, providing a reasonable range of performance from which to differentiate among future test takers. Anastasi (1988) suggests maximum differentiation among test takers can be achieved with items at the 50% difficulty level; however, given that we are focused on classification rather than selection, 70% may be sufficient (Ghiselli et al., 1981). An important next step is testing the items on the specific target groups for classification; scale scores in the pilot test sample were negatively skewed, and the sample population was older and more educated than the population for which the assessment was designed. When applied to the target population - incoming Army officers - scores may be more evenly distributed and show even greater differentiation between respondents.

Study 2 results found seven items in the Systems Thinking assessment that did not discriminate at all among participants, as all participants responded correctly. In addition, on 14 items, participants selected only one of the distractor response options. Because the current sample is very small and not highly similar to the target population, it is not clear whether these items will perform differently with the target population. For the seven items that all pilot test participants answered correctly, it may be that these seven items will be able to distinguish among officers at the lower end of the distribution. After further testing, if the distribution of response option use remains limited for the 14 items, some distractors should be replaced with more enticing options. Similarly, if the seven items continue to show no differentiation among respondents, they should be revised or dropped.

Pilot test data suggested that both the Type 1 and Type 2 items are measuring the same construct, as there were no notable differences in how participants scored on these types of items and the item total correlations overlapped. Future research should examine the internal consistency of the scale and determine if the final scale should include items from Type 1, Type 2, or a mixture of the best performing items from the two item types.

Problem Solver

The SME ratings in Study 1 showed a moderate level of support for the construct validity of the Problem Solver measurement approach. Responses indicated there may be some aspects of the Problem Solver construct, as defined, that are not captured in the measurement approach. One aspect of the construct that SMEs identified as potentially missing from the measure is "constructing" a representation of the problem; in the current measurement individuals must recognize an appropriate representation for a problem, but do not actually "construct" one themselves. The decision to provide participants with representations and have them select the best option instead of allowing participants to freely generate problem representations was made to ensure test delivery and scoring was feasible and practical. Although it would be ideal to allow participants to generate their own representations, this strategy would be extremely difficult to score in an automated manner. Another aspect of the construct that an SME noted as potentially lacking from the measure was "identifying approaches to solve a problem," which is stated in the definition. The SME noted that the test items ask the individual to identify the "best" approach to solve a problem, rather than just identifying various approaches to solve the problem. While the ideal approach to measure this might require participants to generate multiple approaches to solve a problem that is presented to them, this type of constructed response would also be very difficult to capture and score in an automated manner. Given these practical limitations, no changes are recommended to the measure based on the Study 1 results.

The Problem Solver measure appeared to be more challenging for participants than the Systems Thinking measure, with 64% recorded as the highest score achieved. This level of difficulty is suggested to be appropriate to reveal clear differentiation among test takers (e.g., Anastasi, 1988; Ghiselli et al., 1981), and the distribution of scores had sufficient variability to differentiate high and low performers.

While the majority of the items in this measure demonstrated item total correlations that were negative and small in magnitude, it is important to recognize that Problem Solver is more similar to a formative measure, in which each item adds to understanding the construct, rather than a reflective one where each item is driven by an underlying latent factor. Instead of reflecting the latent construct, the breadth of Problem Solver items forms a composite construct with a variety of problem-solving Approaches or Representation items. Successful problem solving requires possessing a breadth of knowledge, and conceptually the items were striving to represent a broad spectrum of types of problems that may be encountered. As such, lower correlations among items would be desirable for this measure. Because the majority of the item total correlations were nonsignificant due to the very small sample size, speculation regarding the negative direction of the correlations is not worthwhile at this time; however, it could potentially suggest that being good at one type of problem approach or representation actually interferes with success in another type of approach or representation.

Generally, the response option distractors seemed to perform well at posing viable alternatives. However, there were two Problem Solver items in the Approaches subscale that all participants answered correctly, with no participants selecting any of the distractors. There were also two items (one Approaches and one Representation) that no participants answered correctly. For one of these (Item 3), 17 participants selected the same distractor option as the correct response. Upon reviewing the item content, it was determined that this was an item that had

29

engendered significant discussion and modification in order to obtain consensus among the SME raters during development and scoring. Together, the challenges during development and the poor item results suggest an inherent problem with the item and response options, so the item was recommended for removal. There were three other items (Items 5, 23, and 34) for which one response option dominated and few or no participants responded to the item correctly. These items should be reexamined carefully after further testing with the actual target population to determine if any changes are needed to the item or response options. Again, because the current sample is very small and not highly similar to the target population, it seems most prudent to wait until additional data has been collected before making other changes.

Once additional data is collected, item difficulties and response option performance should be reviewed and items with very high and very low difficulties could potentially benefit from modifications. For items that are too difficult, response options could be adjusted to make distractors less tempting. In the end, our objective is to identify 12 items each for Approaches and Representation that can discriminate well among individuals. Using the current data, for the Approaches scale, if 6 items with the highest difficulty (Items 3, 5, 12, and 15) and lowest difficulty (Items 7 and 18) are dropped, the difficulties of the remaining items range from 37% to 89%, with an average difficulty of 61% across the remaining 12 items. For Representation, if items with the highest difficulty (Item 23, 30, 34, 36) and lowest difficulty (Items 25, 31) are dropped, the difficulties would range from 37% to 79%, with an average difficulty of 65% across the remaining 12 items. Therefore, the overall potential of the items was strong in discriminating among participants and suggest promise once additional testing can be conducted.

Multitasking

In Study 1, SME ratings of the construct validity of Multitasking were moderately high, with five of the seven raters indicating the measurement approach was "very appropriate," and only two indicating it was "somewhat appropriate." Minor concerns expressed included whether the time constraints of the measure would increase test taker anxiety and reduce construct validity, and whether there was too much overlap in the Primary and Distractor tasks since they both involve reading and searching for information. Regarding the time constraint issue, having time pressure is necessary to ensure that task switching costs are revealed. Without time pressure, the test taker could slow down to deal with the impact of task switching. Test takers would achieve 100 percent accuracy across the board but would do so at different rates. Providing the calibration sequence at the beginning of the assessment, however, should serve to standardize effects of time pressure based on differing reaction times; the calibration ensures that the assessment progresses at an appropriate pace for each test taker. In addition, given that Army officers often operate under time constraints when multitasking, this is not an inappropriate set of environmental conditions for the assessment.

Regarding the overlap between the Primary and Distractor tasks, although both tasks do involve visual search and some degree of reading, the content simply needs to differ enough that the Distractor task would distract the test taker and affect their performance on the Primary task as they mentally switch between the two. It is true that more complex tasks can produce greater switching costs, some degree of switching cost is typically found for any task switching or multitasking (Rogers & Monsell, 1995; Rubinstein et al., 2001). Although a numerical task could be used for one of the tasks, one of our parameters in the assessment development was to

30

not have the content be mathematical or technical. Another option could be some type of graphic or pictorial task. As discussed in the results of Study 2, 73% of the participants showed a performance decrement of 10-20% on Multitasking, suggesting that the Distractor was providing a distraction; the question of whether the distraction is sufficient is an empirical one and is discussed further with respect to the Study 2 results. No changes to the items were recommended specifically based on the Study 1 results.

Study 2 results showed that the first measurement approach, which measured multitasking through comparison of the baseline performance to the interrupted performance, operated as expected, with most participants showing at least a 10% decrement in performance with the addition of interruptions. These results suggest that this general approach to measuring Multitasking is potentially effective; we were able to identify a performance decrement due to the Distractor task, and though variability was small, there was differentiation among participants in the performance decrement.

The second scoring approach was less effective in detecting a decrement, although there was still some variability. In the second approach, a performance decrement was examined by comparing performance immediately before and immediately after an interruption from the Distractor task. Investigating the calibration item data in further detail revealed that a programming code was impacting the test calibration assignments: average times on the calibration items were set to always round up, which meant that participants were consistently placed into tests that had slightly longer time limits than their average calibration item times. This had the consequence of making the test slightly easier for them. It would be potentially more useful to have the program consistently round down. Further, in three cases, the rounding program created a difference of more than one second and participants were placed in a group one second slower than their specified group. Specifically, the average times of 7.85, 7.75, and 5.97 seconds resulted in time limits of 9, 9, and 7 seconds rather than 8, 8, and 6 seconds, respectively. These rounding differences are problematic because they reduce the amount of time pressure in the Primary task, making the task too easy to accomplish.

Upon further investigation, another problem with the calibration choices for Multitasking was the default use of average response latencies to provide an estimate of the participant's required response time without taking into consideration two other factors: (a) the variability around participants' response latencies, and (b) the response time needed to reach the desired level of average performance, which is somewhat less than 100 percent. In the present data, the standard deviation around the mean calibration item response latency was 2.28, on average, which represents a 3-second change when rounded up. For items as simple as the Primary task items, that is a significant amount of extra time. In addition, this variability is somewhat predictable, in that despite the initial practice problems that the participant was given, the first couple calibration items consistently took the longest and test takers' speed increased on the latter three items. As an illustration, 15 participants responded slower on the first calibration item than their subsequent time limit category, but calibration items three, four, and five were slower than the time limit category only eight times. This issue also placed individuals in a calibration category that was be too easy. It can be avoided in the future by developing a specialized administration platform that dynamically adjust the time limits based on performance and/or stage of the test. The current Multitasking test used 10 pre-configured time limits and test takers were assigned one of those for the duration of the test. An adaptive test could be programmed,

31

however, to adjust the time limits in real time to modify the time pressure exerted. If future administrations of the assessment use calibration categories rather than adjusting dynamically, the average calibration time should be programmed to discount the first couple of items or take the fastest response time as the basis for assigning time limits.

The other factor that needs to be taken into consideration is the desired level of average performance. As with other measurement, the Multitasking measure will achieve maximum differentiation when difficulty is between 50% and 70%. As mentioned above, Primary task performance averaged 86 percent (SD = 5 percent) in the present research. For Multitasking specifically, where the Primary task items are not particularly difficult to answer, it is important to apply time pressure so that the effects of the Interruption task can be detected. Test takers should fail on items a certain percent of the time due to the time limit. An average 70 percent success rate across trials would likely produce sufficient variability in performance. In the present data, the time limit was reached 40 times out of 1919, or about 2 percent of trials. Together, this information suggests that the time limits should be reduced substantially to improve the ability of the measure to discriminate among participants. In future iterations, participants should be instructed to expect to get timed out on some of the questions and the time pressure should be increased. Again, a dynamic approach to establishing timing, or if that is not feasible, taking the average of the three fastest calibration times or even just using the minimum time, would be more appropriate for setting time limit assignments.

Finally, it is possible that using a Distractor task that was less similar to the Primary task (e.g., engaging in a graphic or pictorial task that differed more from the Primary reading comprehension and visual searching task) would require a higher degree of task switching and therefore increase the level of performance decrement in some participants. Further exploration of the specific difficulty of the tasks should be conducted using a sample population that is closely aligned with the target population. Once working with the appropriate target population, it can more appropriately be determined whether it would be beneficial to make the Distractor task more difficult or more dissimilar to the Primary task in order to see greater performance decrements.

Conclusions

While the investigation into the validity of Systems Thinking, Problem Solver, and Multitasking was very preliminary, results suggest each measure shows potential. Each of the assessments needs to be tested on the target population to evaluate the difficulty and discrimination capability of the measures specifically for the target population. Systems Thinking demonstrated appropriate discrimination in the pilot test; while some of the distractor response options may need to be altered for individual items to be most effective, if the Type 1 and Type 2 items are indeed reflecting a single Systems Thinking construct, there may be a sufficient number of strong items already and weaker items can simply be dropped. Problem Solver also demonstrated a strong ability to discriminate among participants. Although one item was recommended for deletion, there are a sufficient number of strong items remaining that the measure is also ready for testing on the target population. Results regarding Multitasking suggest the measure was successful in creating a performance decrement but several modifications to the measure that could produce even more effective discrimination were also identified. It should be noted that while the Systems Thinking and Problem Solver constructs can be measured using any platform that hosts multiple choice questions, including paper-based formats, the Multitasking measure has more unique hosting and development requirements and will require some degree of tailoring to fit the host assessment platform.

Future research is needed to examine the reliability and validity of the assessments within the target population of new Army officers. This includes evaluating convergent and discriminant validity, as well as criterion-related validity and exploring the capability of the measures to classify officers for various branch assignments.

References

Anastasi, A. (1988). *Psychological testing.* Macmillan Publishing Company.

Ghiselli, E. E., Campbell, J. P., & Zedeck, S. (1981). *Measurement theory for the behavioral sciences.* W.H. Freeman and Company.

Rogers, R. & Monsell, S. (1995). The costs of a predictable switch between simple cognitive tasks. *Journal of Experimental Psychology: General, 124*(2), 207-231. https://doi.org/ 10.1037/0096-3445.124.2.207

Rubinstein, J. S., Meyer, D. E. & Evans, J. E. (2001). Executive Control of Cognitive Processes in Task Switching. *Journal of Experimental Psychology: Human Perception and Performance, 27*(4)*,* 763-797. https://doi.org/ 10.1037/0096-1523.27.4.763

U.S. Army TRADOC G-2. (February, 2019). *Decisive Action Training Environment.* U.S. Army TRADOC G-2 ACE Threats Integration. https://odin.tradoc.army.mil/DATEWORLD

Wisecarver. M, Adis, C., Glorioso. M., Byrd, C., Engelsted, L., Martin, J. (in preparation). *Innovative Cognitive Assessment for Officer Classification* (Technical Report). U.S. Army Research Institute for the Behavioral and Social Sciences.

Appendix A

Systems Thinking Measure Details

Construct: Systems Thinking	**Subdimensions:** None

Source (ATAF) Definition:

Conceptualizes and understands relationships and arrangements within and between relevant components and structures

Operational Definition:

Conceptualizes and understands relationships and arrangements within and between relevant components and structures

Measurement Overview: Test taker will respond to multiple choice items that describe the relationships between/among elements of a system and demonstrate their understanding of the relationships and dynamics in the system. Test taker will view a static image/graphic or read a text description that describes a fictitious system, then select the image/graphic or text description that corresponds to the system. System characteristics will be modeled after a variety of system types (i.e., biological, mechanical, social, etc.), but the assessment will be designed such that existing knowledge of specific systems is not required.

Measure Details:

Description:

- Item Type 1: Test taker will read a text description of a system and select the best graphical representation of the relationships in that system

- Item Type 2: Test taker will be presented with a graphic model or image of a complex system and be asked to select the multiple-choice response option that best describes the graphical system

Scoring:

Scores are based on total correct responses.

This scoring strategy could be administered in CAT framework to reduce item exposure and testing time while increasing the precision of the ability estimate.

Example Items:

1. Traffic on the highways around national holidays can be quite an obstacle. Over the decades, the traffic has become heavier with an increased number of cars on the roads. It is now to the point where many people do not bother to travel on holidays anymore and just stay home. Which of the following diagrams best represents this situation?

Response Options:

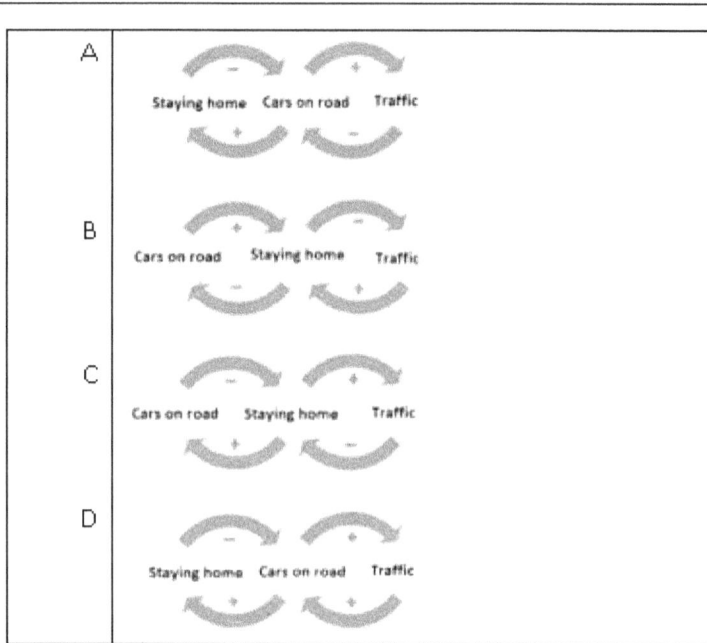

Correct Response: B

2. The model below shows relationships among three components. Which of the descriptions listed below best represents the model?

LEN   ACE   DRG

Response Options:
   a.   The more LEN there is, the more ACE there is likely to be. DRG decreases the release of ACE and LEN, so when there is more DRG, there is likely to be less ACE and LEN.
   b.   LEN causes the release of ACE. ACE causes the release of DRG. DRG causes the release of LEN.
   c.   The less LEN there is, the more ACE there is likely to be. DRG increases the release of ACE and LEN, so when there is more DRG, there is likely to be more ACE and LEN.
   d.   LEN decreases the release of ACE. ACE increases the release of DRG. DRG increases the release of LEN.

Correct Response: A

Appendix B

Problem Solver Measure Details

Constructs: Problem Solver	**Subdimensions:** Representations, Approaches

Source (ATAF) Definition:

Problem Solver: A capacity to choose between best practices and unorthodox approaches to reach a solution; accomplishes the task.

Operational Definition:

Problem Solver: Understands multiple approaches for representing and solving problems.

Representations: Knowledge of and skill in forming external representations of an ill-defined problem.

Approaches: Knowledge of and skill in identifying methods and plans for solving problems.

Measurement Overview: A multiple-choice test of general problem-solving knowledge and skills, consisting of items measuring both dimensions. Scenario-based stems will be used to frame the questions.

Measure Details:

Description:

- Representation Items: Test takers are asked to identify the best external representation of a problem given a goal (e.g., reframing, communicating, understanding the problem). Correct answers are verifiably correct based on prescriptions in the literature for creating external representations and visualizations.
- Approaches Items: Test takers are asked to identify the best approach for either solving or making progress toward solving a problem. Approaches items may also deal with formulating a plan based on chosen methods for solving a problem. Correct answers are determined based on both prescriptions in the literature and SME consensus.

Scoring:

Each item is scored as correct or not correct and total scores are based on the average across all items.

This assessment could be administered in CAT framework to reduce item exposure and testing time, while increasing the precision of the ability estimate.

Example Items:

Representations:

Each week, a person of interest goes out to a rendezvous point, meets with a contact, then returns home the next day. The person of interest always follows the same path to and from the rendezvous point and the trips always take the same amount of time. You want to determine if there is a place along the path that the person reaches at the same time on both the trip out and the trip back, so you can form a plan for intercepting information from the person's mobile phone.

1. What is the best way to show this problem to come to a quick solution?
    A. With a short, descriptive paragraph laying out all the considerations in the scenario
    B. With a pair of overlapping circles representing the trip out and the trip back

B-1

C. With a table of locations along the path and the times those locations are typically reached

D. With a pair of overlapping line graphs showing location on path by time of day

Correct response: D

Approaches:

2. A new system is malfunctioning without an apparent cause. All the following approaches are valid ways to solve a problem, but which one would work best in the above scenario?

A. Work backward from the goal to determine the issue

B. Think of an analogy or metaphor for the problem

C. Leave the problem alone for a while, then come back to it later

D. Guess at what the problem is and run a test to confirm

Correct response: TBD

Appendix C

Multitasking

Measurement Details	
Construct: Multitasking	**Subdimensions:** None

Source (ATAF) Definition:

Rapidly processes and prioritizes multiple demands simultaneously; Takes appropriate action when multiple stimuli compete for his or her attention.

Operational Definition:

The ability to shift attention between two or more tasks with minimal reduction in performance.

Measurement Overview: Test takers complete a visual search task to establish a baseline score, then complete the same task while interruptive prompts are occurring to measure the level of performance decrement due to shifting tasks.

Measure Details:

Description:

Test takers will first be provided with a visual search task where they are asked to select Soldiers with certain characteristics or qualifications from a list so that these Soldiers can be assigned to a special unit. Test takers are provided with a table that lists Soldiers and descriptions of certain characteristics such as MOS, rank, and time-in-grade, as well as a set of rules regarding how the selections should be made. In order to prevent an increase in performance due to memorization of Soldier qualifications, for each new item, a new list of Soldiers with different qualifications will be provided or the names in the list will be shuffled and names already used will be replaced. Test takers will be asked to select the appropriate Soldiers by double clicking the names that meet the stated requirements. Test takers are given 10 seconds per item to find the appropriate Soldiers before the test advances to the next item. To increase variance, each list will contain multiple names that meet the requirements, requiring test takers to identify as many appropriately qualified Soldiers as they can within the timeframe.

An initial set of 8-12 items will be completed without interruption tasks and will serve as the baseline for performance. The number of items in the initial set will be determined based on the amount of time each item takes to process, with a goal of achieving a baseline time-period of around two minutes. After establishing a baseline score, test takers will complete another set of approximately 28 items, but this time will also receive interruption tasks every 3-5 items. These tasks will be in the form of pop-up windows made to look like messages from a colleague or superior asking for information about a Soldier (e.g., whether they are deployable or what their specific qualifications are) or general information about the set of Soldiers (e.g., are there at least five deployable Infantry Soldiers in your current list?). For these tasks it will be necessary to ensure the test taker is able to look at the list of Soldiers so that they do not have to rely on working memory to answer the questions.

Test takers will provide a Yes/No response to the interruption task, then return to the visual search task. While the interruption task is on screen, only the table from the visual search task will be visible – not the Soldier specification directions used to make the selections for the special unit, and the test taker will not be able to engage in selecting responses for the visual search task. The interruption task will remain on screen until it has been answered or 10 seconds has passed (time to be determined), whichever comes first.

C-1

At that time, the next visual search task item will appear. For the trial to count, the test taker must answer the interruption task correctly. Additional items are added for each incorrect response. The test ends four items after the participant answers five interruption tasks correctly.

Scoring:

Formula or Sensitivity Metric

Scores are based on search performance, using either a formula scoring approach that adds points for each correct click (hits) and subtracts points for each incorrect click (false alarms) or a sensitivity metric like d-prime which accounts for hits, misses, false alarms, and correct rejections. If a sensitivity metric is used, several correct selections will be required per table. Two scores -a baseline and a Multitasking score- are calculated as follows:

1. Baseline Score - An initial set of 8-12 items will be completed without interruptions and will serve as the baseline for performance. Responses will be scored based on the number correct. Test takers can achieve partial credit by selecting only some of the correct Soldiers for the special unit, which should increase the range of scores and help differentiate between high and low performers more effectively. An overall score for the initial items is calculated as the baseline score.
2. Multitasking Score – A second set of items will be completed with periodic interruptions that must be addressed before the test taker can return to the original task. Responses will be scored using the same procedure as the baseline. An overall score for the interruption trials is calculated and the performance decrement between the baseline and Multitasking conditions is used to calculate the final Multitasking score. A smaller performance decrement between the Multitasking and the baseline conditions would result in a higher final Multitasking score.

Example Items:

(Primary Task)

For this task, you are being asked to assign Soldiers to special units based on their qualifications. For each question you will be provided with the specific requirements for that special unit and a table of Soldiers from which to choose. You must examine the requirements for the special unit and then select the Soldiers that meet the requirements by double-clicking on their name in the table.

As you complete this task, you may receive messages from various coworkers asking for specific information about the Soldiers in the table. Please respond to these messages immediately and to the best of your ability, then continue with the special unit assignment task.

This task will take between 5-10 minutes.

Please select all Soldiers in Roster 1 who have a rank of 1LT and MOS of 11A. [Correct responses can be seen in bold.]

Roster 1				
Soldier	**MOS**	**Rank**	**Time in Grade**	**Deployable**
1. **Gonzalez**	**11A**	**1LT**	**6 months**	**No**
2. Kim	12A	LTC	12 months	Yes
3. Graham	25A	CPT	18 months	No

4. Mendez	25A	CPT	6 months	Yes
5. Lee	19A	1LT	12 months	Yes
6. Bertram	**11A**	**1LT**	**18 months**	**Yes**
7. Williams	12A	MAJ	12 months	Yes
8. Johnson	17A	CPT	18 months	No
9. Ramirez	**11A**	**1LT**	**12 months**	**No**
10. Patel	25A	CPT	6 months	Yes
11. Jones	**11A**	**1LT**	**12 months**	**Yes**
12. Becker	12A	MAJ	6 months	No

(Interruption task)

Please select the check box next to any lines that contain repeat words.

Over 200,000 square miles comprise the **Caucasus, Caucasus,** a
mountainous region **located located** between the Black Sea
and the Caspian Sea. The Caucasus includes
Atropia, Limaria, and Gorgas, as **well well** as parts of
Ariana and Donovia. The Caucasus Mountains,
consisting of the Greater and Lesser Caucasus
ranges, traditionally form the separation between
Europe and Asia. The Caucasus region contains two
major parts—the **North North** Caucasus and the South

Appendix D

Item Results Summary Tables

Table D1

Systems Thinking Item Type 1 Results Summary Table

Type 1 Item	Correlation with Overall Score	% Participants Scoring Correctly	Number of Response Options Used
ST 1	.53	79%	3
ST 2	.41	74%	3
ST 3	.65	74%	4
ST 4	--	100%	1
ST 5	.13	89%	2
ST 6	--	100%	1
ST 7	-.03	89%	2
ST 8	.53	74%	2
ST 9	.60	74%	3
ST 10	.44	68%	3
ST 11	.55	63%	3
ST 12	.65	89%	2
ST 13	.13	63%	4
ST 14	.52	58%	4
ST 15	.75	74%	2
ST 16	--	100%	1
ST 17	.58	63%	2
ST 18	.54	84%	2

Table D2

Systems Thinking Item Type 2 Results Summary Table

Type 2 Item	Correlation with Overall Score	% Participants Scoring Correctly	Number of Response Options Used
ST 19	-.36	42%	3
ST 20	.56	84%	2
ST 21	.21	74%	2
ST 22	.02	95%	2
ST 23	-.26	84%	3
ST 24	--	100%	1
ST 25	--	100%	1
ST 26	.75	47%	4
ST 27	.66	42%	3
ST 28	-.15	95%	2
ST 29	.39	74%	3
ST 30	--	100%	1
ST 31	.48	53%	4
ST 32	.40	84%	2
ST 33	.18	79%	2
ST 34	.65	89%	3
ST 35	.41	95%	2
ST 36	.71	84%	3
ST 37	--	100%	1

D-2

Table D3

Problem Solver Approaches Results Summary Table

Item	Overall Score Correlation	% Participants Scoring Correctly	Number of Response Options Used
PS 1	-.22	74%	2
PS 2	-.10	47%	3
PS 3	--	0%	3
PS 4	-.43	89%	2
PS 5	-.21	21%	2
PS 6	.38	37%	3
PS 7	--	100%	1
PS 8	-.19	89%	2
PS 9	-.49	68%	3
PS 10	-.27	89%	2
PS 11	-.05	42%	3
PS 12	-.09	5%	3
PS 13	-.19	68%	3
PS 14	-.11	37%	4
PS 15	.19	21%	4
PS 16	.12	47%	4
PS 17	-.44	42%	2
PS 18	--	100%	1

Table D4

Problem Solver Representations Results Summary Table

Item	Overall Score Correlation	% Participants Scoring Correctly	Number of Response Options Used
PS 19	.58	68%	2
PS 20	.28	79%	3
PS 21	-.23	58%	3
PS 22	-.25	79%	3
PS 23	-.12	11%	4
PS 24	-.40	63%	3
PS 25	.22	84%	3
PS 26	-.07	58%	2
PS 27	.14	79%	3
PS 28	.43	74%	3
PS 29	-.31	63%	3
PS 30	--	0%	3
PS 31	-.27	89%	2
PS 32	.18	37%	4
PS 33	.38	63%	3
PS 34	-.03	11%	4
PS 35	-.21	63%	2
PS 36	-.39	21%	4

www.ingramcontent.com/pod-product-compliance
Lightning Source LLC
Chambersburg PA
CBHW081201270326
41930CB00014B/3255